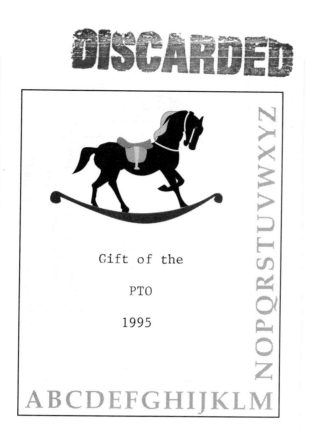

Gift of the

PTO

1995

NOPQRSTUVWXYZ

ABCDEFGHIJKLM

A New True Book

THE SIOUX

By Alice Osinski

CHILDRENS PRESS ™

CHICAGO

Sioux war dance

PHOTO CREDITS

Historical Pictures Service, Chicago—
2 (Rudolf Cronan), 8, 15, 18, 22 (top),
26 (top), 35

Stock Boston—© John Running, 44 (left), 45

Holiday Film Corporation—4 (top)

© Tom Stack—39 (left)

© Jacqueline Durand—39 (right),
41 (2 photos), 44 (right)

Nawrocki Stock Photo:
© Brian Seed and W.S. Nawrocki—4,
6 (2 photos), 9 (3 photos), 36
© 1982 W.S. Nawrocki—14, 24 (2 photos),
25 (2 photos), 26 (bottom), 30 (2 photos),
31 (middle), 37, 38 (4 photos)

South Dakota State Historical Society—16,
28

South Dakota Division of Tourism—40

Lynn M. Stone—22 (bottom)

Wyoming Travel Co.—Cover, 43 (bottom)

Reinhard Brucker—13, 29 (2 photos),
31 (2 photos, left and right), 32, 43

Stanley J. Morrow Collection, W.H. Over
Museum, S.D.—19, 20

Len Meents—11

COVER—Sioux powwow in Wyoming

Lakotas of Pine Ridge, "pilamaye" *(Sioux word for "thank you")*

Library of Congress Cataloging in Publication Data

Osinski, Alice.
  The Sioux.

  (A New true book)
  Includes index.
  Summary: A brief history of the Sioux, or Dakota,
Indians of the Great Plains describing their tribal
organization, customs, religion, and their encounter
with the white settlers.
  1. Dakota Indians—Juvenile literature. [1. Dakota
Indians. 2. Indiana of North America] I. Title.
E99.D1084   1984   978'.00497   84-7629
ISBN 0-516-01929-5   AACR2

EIGHTH PRINTING 1992
Copyright © 1984 by Regensteiner Publishing Enterprises, Inc.
All rights reserved. Published simultaneously in Canada.
Printed in the United States of America.

11 12 13 14 15 16 17 18 19 20 R 02 01 00 99 98 97 96 95 94

TABLE OF CONTENTS

Edwin E. "Buzz" Aldrin (above) was the second human to step on the moon.

Photograph of Long Hand and his family (right) taken in 1911 at Fort Yates, North Dakota

4

THE FIRST AMERICANS

Neil Armstrong and Edwin E. "Buzz" Aldrin, Jr., were the first Americans to explore the moon. Do you know who were the first explorers in America? You may think Christopher Columbus was the first, but he was not. The Indians were the first explorers. They explored North America for thousands of years before Columbus landed.

Photograph of Sitting Bull
and his family (above)
taken by S.T. Fanser.
This close-up of
Sitting Bull (right) was
taken by G.W. Scott at
Fort Yates, North Dakota.

6

HOW THE SIOUX CAME TO THE GREAT PLAINS

Sitting Bull is the name of a famous Indian. He was one of the leaders of a proud Indian tribe called the Sioux.

The Sioux once lived in the area that is now Minnesota. About three hundred years ago most of them moved west to the Great Plains. Dogs helped them carry their belongings on the long journey.

Frederic Remington's illustration of the Indian method of breaking a pony. Horses were brought to North America by explorers from Europe.

On their way west, the Sioux acquired wild horses and learned to ride them. Horses helped them to travel farther and hunt more buffalo. By the time

8

Photographs of Gall (far left), Red Cloud (middle), and Rain in
the Face (right), taken by D.F. Barry in the 1880s

the Sioux claimed the land
shown on the map on page
11, they were excellent horse
riders and buffalo hunters.
They were strong warriors,
too. They had become a
great fighting nation.

THE SEVEN COUNCIL FIRES

The Sioux nation had
seven groups. They
called themselves the
Seven Council Fires. The
seven groups shared land
from present-day
Minnesota to Montana
and from Wyoming to
Nebraska. Each Council
Fire had its own leaders
and its own group of
families that always
camped together.

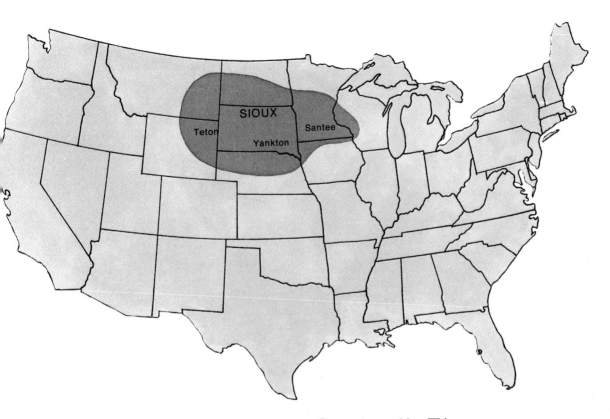

The largest Council Fire
lived on the western plains.
It was so large that it also
was divided into seven
groups—known as the Teton
Sioux. They spoke the Lakota
dialect of the Sioux language. 11

Two councils lived on
the middle plains and were
called Yankton Sioux. They
spoke the Nakota dialect
of the Sioux language. The
other Council Fires lived
on the plains in the east.
They called themselves
Santee Sioux and spoke the
Dakota dialect of the Sioux
language.

The councils lived great
distances from each other,
but they could understand
each other's dialect. Only
the families within each
Council Fire met once a

year during the summer.
When families met, they
shared news and traded
things they had gotten
from other tribes. They
gave gifts at special feasts
called giveaways. They

This toy horse and drum are part of the collection of Sioux toys on display at the South Dakota Cultural Heritage Center in Pierre, South Dakota.

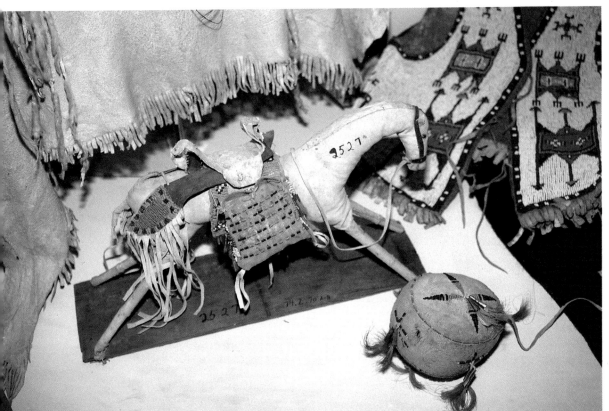

Sioux
pictograph
of the
Sun Dance

played ball games and
raced horses, too. It was
also a time to give thanks
for the past year and ask
for help in the new year.
The people did this by
taking part in a Sun Dance.

SIOUX PONIES

The Sioux never camped
in one place for long. They
were nomads who moved
their camps to follow the
buffalo herds and to find
fresh grass for their ponies.

15

1891 photograph by Grabill called "Villa of Brule." The Sioux spent most of their lives on horseback. By the age of three, children were riding with their mothers. At five or six, a boy might have his own horse.

Everyone placed a high value on horses. A family was wealthy if it had many

ponies. When a good horse
died, it was like losing
a friend. Sometimes horses
owned by other tribes would
be kept in a family lodge
to prevent them from being
stolen by skillful Sioux
raiders. Most tribes on
the plains stole horses
from their enemies. That
was one way they made
their herds bigger. Men
needed good horses. They
spent a lot of time training
them for hunting and for war.

"Moving Camp" drawn by De Cost Smith

Horses also were used
when camps had to move.
Families carried belongings
on the backs of horses.
They also put children, old
people, and other belongings
on a platform that a horse
pulled. The platform was
called a travois.

Sioux tipi among willows. The Sioux had favorite spots on rivers where they returned every year.

CAMP CIRCLES

New camps were set up near water and wooded areas. Trees protected the people and provided wood for making fires. During most of the year, the Sioux had favorite places to camp in river valleys surrounding the Black Hills. The Black Hills

19

Buffalo hides were used to make tipis, robes, and moccasins. The Sioux hunted deer, antelope, buffalo, and other animals in the Black Hills.

were used for gatherings and religious ceremonies.

Camps were made in circles. Tipis were put up and taken down by the women. They were the best kind of houses for people on the move. They

Sioux tipi at a modern-day powwow

were made from buffalo hides and poles. Although tipis were very light, they could hold up against strong winds. They were waterproof, too. Tipis were warm in winter and cool in summer. When fires were lighted inside, special holes let the smoke out.

Sioux hunters used animal skins (above) to hide their scent when stalking buffalo. Every part of the buffalo was used to feed and clothe the tribe. Nothing was wasted. The death of a buffalo meant life for the Sioux.

THE GIFT OF THE BUFFALO

Life was hard on the plains. Being brave was important. Fighting enemies and hunting buffalo were dangerous events. If hunters were not careful, they could be attacked. Some buffalo stood six feet tall and weighed two thousand pounds each. Before the Sioux had horses, they hunted the buffalo on foot.

Toy tipi

Man's jacket

Almost everything the Sioux needed for living on the plains came from the buffalo. Every part of the animal was used. Nothing was wasted. Food, clothing, tipis, toys, cooking items, weapons, tools, thread,

24

Indian leather doll (left) with human hair, wearing
leather beaded dress. Bone knife (right)

paintbrushes, soap, glue,
and fuel were all made
from the buffalo. Because
the Sioux believed the
buffalo and other animals
were sacred, special prayers
were said before hunting
and killing them.

Frederic Remington drew this prayer scene called "Facing the Setting Sun."
Special pipes (below) and special prayers were used in Sioux ceremonies.

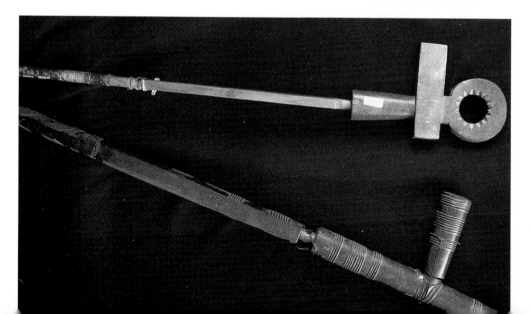

PRAYING TO THE GREAT SPIRIT

Prayer was an important part of Sioux life. They believed Wakan Tanka or the Great Spirit had power over all things. Prayers were said and songs were sung to the Great Spirit. Often sacred pipes were smoked to help their prayers be heard. Sometimes people prayed together in places

Photograph of a Sioux "sweat lodge" taken in 1898 by J.H. Bratley of the Lower Cut Meat Creek Camp School, Rosebud Reservation, South Dakota

called sweat lodges. Other times, people went off into the hills to pray alone.

A few people were taught to cure the sick. These medicine men and women

Sioux rattles   Sioux headdress

knew which plants to use
for colds, toothaches, or
broken bones. Special songs
and special ceremonies
were used to heal.

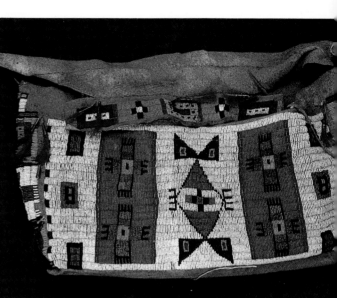

Women's beaded dress   Tipi bag

FEATHERS AND BEADS

Sioux belongings were
made with beautiful
designs and colors. Painted
tipis, robes, and shields
told of brave deeds and

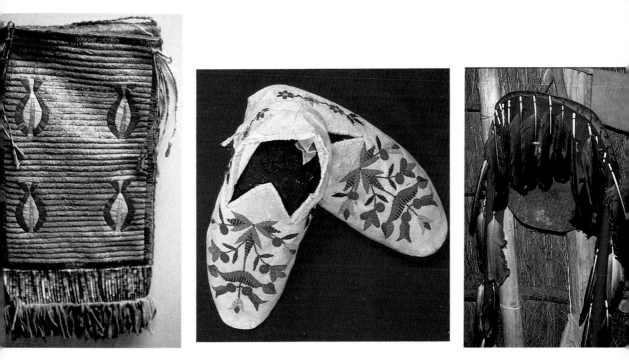

Bead and porcupine quill bag (left), beaded moccasins (middle), shield (right)

special dreams. Warriors
painted their bodies and
their horses before going
to war. Women made
things with porcupine quills
and beads. Shells and
eagle feathers were used,

Hide painting

too. Each tribe had its own
special design.

Some painting was done
only by men who kept the
history of the tribe. The
Sioux did not write their
language down. Instead,

they painted little figures on rawhide. Each figure stood for an important event in the life of the tribe. The painting was called a winter count because it was done every year in the winter.

People used the winter count to retell events. Through storytelling, their history was remembered. It was the way old people passed their memories and traditions on to the young.

FIGHTING FOR THE LAND

When white settlers
began moving into Sioux
land, there were many
battles. The Sioux believed
land should be shared, not
owned. The settlers wanted
to own land and use it for
farming and for ranching.
They wanted to take gold
from the Black Hills.

The United States Army
was sent to keep the
Sioux away from the
settlers. Sometimes the

The Battle of the Little Bighorn, or
Custer's Last Stand, was fought in 1876.

army attacked Sioux
camps. The Sioux fought
back to protect their
families and their way of
life. They fought to keep
the land.

One famous battle took
place in 1876. The Sioux
and another tribe, the

First row: Bill Halsey and Sitting Bull. Second row: Crow King and Buffalo Bill. Photograph taken before 1890 by William Notman and Son

Cheyenne, were camped along the Little Bighorn River by the Bighorn Mountains in present-day Montana. George A. Custer and his troops attacked them. The Indians fought back. Although the Sioux won this battle, their land was taken from them later.

Oglala Boarding School photograph taken in 1914 at Pine Ridge, South Dakota. The girl marked with an X (second from left) is Nancy Sitting Bull, the grandchild of the famous Sioux chief.

The last fight between the Sioux and the United States Army was at Wounded Knee, South Dakota, in 1890. When this unfortunate battle was over, the Sioux were put on reservations—land kept for Indians.

Music room (top left), carpenter's class (left), and fourth grade classroom (right) at the Agricultural Boarding School Standing Rock Agency (reservation) in North Dakota. Sioux Indian band (top right) at Fort Yates, North Dakota, photographed by Fuller and Fansler

There were no buffalo to hunt on reservations. Camp life changed. The Sioux were forced to speak a new language and learn a new way of life.

THE MODERN SIOUX

Today the Sioux live a
modern way of life. But the
modern way is joined with
the ways of the past. The
Sioux are citizens of the
United States. But they

keep the traditions of their tribe, too. Although many Sioux live in cities, most still live on reservations.

Horses are no longer used for travel or for war. Today, Indians ride horses in rodeos and for fun. Buffalo are not hunted. They are protected

Sioux cowboy and clown at South Dakota rodeo

Sioux traditions continue to be passed from one generation to the next.

in state parks and on land owned by the tribe.

Traditional dancing and singing are still very important. Gatherings, called powwows, bring different tribes together from all parts of the United States and Canada. The best singers and dancers compete for a prize. The Sun Dance is still danced, too. At the Sun Dance, traditional prayers are offered in thanksgiving for health or for individual needs.

Sioux hide painting by Paha Ska (above) is on display at the
Crazy Horse Museum in Crazy Horse, South Dakota. Every year
powwows featuring Native American dances and songs are held
throughout North America (below).

As more Sioux enter professions, such as surveyors (left) and architects (right), reservation life will improve.

Modern life is hard for Sioux Americans. There are few jobs for them on reservations. They face many problems in the cities. It is not easy to hold on to the old ways and live as other Americans

44

do. Perhaps someday the two ways of living will not be so different. More people are learning to appreciate Indian ways. They realize that the first Americans knew how to enjoy their families and use the land wisely.

45

WORDS YOU SHOULD KNOW

buffalo (BUFF • uh • loh) — the wild ox that lived on the Great Plains

ceremony (SEHR • uh • moh • nee) — an act or group of acts that follow traditions

council (KOWN • suhl) — a meeting for discussing things or a group of people who discuss things and give advice

count — an old form of record keeping; a telling of events that have happened

Dakota (duh • KOH • tuh) — a North American Indian dialect

design (di • ZINE) — a pattern used to decorate something

dialect (DYE • uh • lekt) — a regional variety of a language having vocabulary, grammar, and pronunciation that are different from other varieties of the language

explore (ek • SPLOR) — to travel in new and different places in order to find out what they are like

history (HISS • ter • ee) — the story of events that have happened in the past

Lakota (luh • KOH • tuh) — a North American Indian dialect

lodge — a place used by North American Indians for meetings. Some kinds of Indian living places are also called lodges.

memories (MEM • uh • reez) — things, people, and happenings that are remembered

Nakota (nuh • KOH • tuh) — a North American Indian dialect

nation (NAY • shun) — a group of tribes or people that have joined together

nomad (NOH • mad) — an individual or group that moves from place to place to find food for both the people and the animals

powwow (POW • wow) — a North American Indian gathering that usually includes feasting, dancing, and singing

quill — a stiff, sharp-pointed growth that sticks out of some animals' bodies for protection

rawhide (RAW • hide) — animal skin that has not been treated with tannin, which turns it into leather

reservation (rez • er • VAY • shun) — land that has been set apart for a special purpose

rodeo (ROH • dee • oh or roh • DAY • oh) — a show or contest that has bronco riding, calf roping, bull riding, and steer wrestling

sacred (SAY • krid) — holy

Santee (san • TEE) — the four Sioux Council Fires of the eastern plains

settler (SET • ler) — a person who sets up home in a new country

shield — something that is used to protect the body in a battle

Sioux — a North American Indian tribe

sweat — moisture that comes out of the pores, which are tiny openings in the skin

Teton (TEE • tuhn) — the largest Council Fire of the Sioux nation

tipi (TEE • pee) — a cone-shaped tent made of hides, used by the Indians of the Great Plains

tradition (truh • DISH • uhn) — the beliefs, customs, stories, and so on that are handed down from parents to children

travois (truh • VOY or TRAV • oy) — a carrier made up of two trailing poles with a platform stretched between them for the load

tribe — a group of people with the same customs who band together under the same leadership

warrior (WOR • ee • er) — someone with practice and skill in fighting battles

wealthy (WEL • thee) — having riches

weapon (WEP • uhn) — anything that is used in fighting

Yankton (YANK • tuhn) — the two Sioux council fires of the middle plains

INDEX

About the Author

Alice Osinski has had a varied career in the field of education. Her accomplishments include teacher consultant, director of bicultural curriculum and alternative education programs, and producer of educational filmstrips. A seven year teaching experience with the Oglala Sioux of Pine Ridge, SD and Pueblo and Navajo of Gallup, NM helped to launch her career in writing. Ms. Osinski has written several articles about the unique life style of American Indians and has co-authored a filmstrip entitled Grandmother White Loon Feather's Thanksgiving. Ms. Osinski uses a Lakota Sioux expression, which is often said at the completion of a personal prayer, to express her feelings about the writing of this book: "Mitakuye Oyasin" (all my relatives).